Sharks

Stephen Savage

KINGFISHER
NEW YORK

KINGFISHER
LONDON & NEW YORK

Library of Congress Cataloging-in-Publication data
has been applied for.

ISBN: 978-0-7534-5441-1

Kingfisher books are available for special promotions and
premiums. For details contact: Special Markets Department,
Macmillan, 175 Fifth Avenue, New York, NY 10010.

For more information, please visit www.kingfisherbooks.com

First American Edition 2002
Printed in China
20 19 18 17
17TR/0117/WKT/RNB/128MA

Illustrators: Ray Grinaway 10–11, 11*t*, 13*cr*, 15*t*, 18–19, 21*tl*,
23*tr*, 25*tr*, 28–29; **Kevin Maddison** 12–13, 16–17, 26–27;
Michael Rowe 4–5, 8–9, 22–23; **Roger Stewart** 6–7, 14–15,
20–21, 21*cr*, 24–25.
Cartoons: Ian Dicks
Picture acknowledgments: 5*bl* Shutterstock/Laura D,
7*tr* Shutterstock/Matt9122, **10***bl* Shutterstock/Elsa Hoffmann,
14*bl* Seapics/Gwen Lowe, **22***bl* Seapics/Marty Snyderman,
25*cl* Alamy/FLPA, **27***tr* Seapics/Marty Snyderman, **29***tr* Ardea/
Kurt Amsler.

CONTENTS

4 WHAT is a shark?

6 WHERE do sharks live?

8 HOW can a shark drown?

10 HOW many rows of teeth do sandtiger sharks have?

12 WHAT is a great white shark's favorite food?

14 HOW big is the whale shark?

16 WHY are people frightened of sharks?

18 WHICH shark can smell blood 2.5 miles away?

20 WHY are most sharks gray and white?

22 WHICH shark has a hammer?

24 HOW are lemon sharks born?

26 WHY do pilot fish live with sharks?

28 WHO eats sharks?

30 SHARKS QUIZ

31 GLOSSARY

32 INDEX

ABOUT this book

Have you ever wondered how many types of sharks there are? Have all your questions about sharks answered, and learn other fascinating facts on every information-packed page of this book. Words in **bold** are in the glossary on page 31.

Look and find ★ ★ mouth

All through the book, you will see the **Look and find** symbol. This has the name and picture of a small object that is hidden somewhere on the page. Look carefully to see if you can find it.

Now I know . . .

★ These boxes contain quick answers to all of the questions.

★ They will help you remember all about the amazing world of sharks.

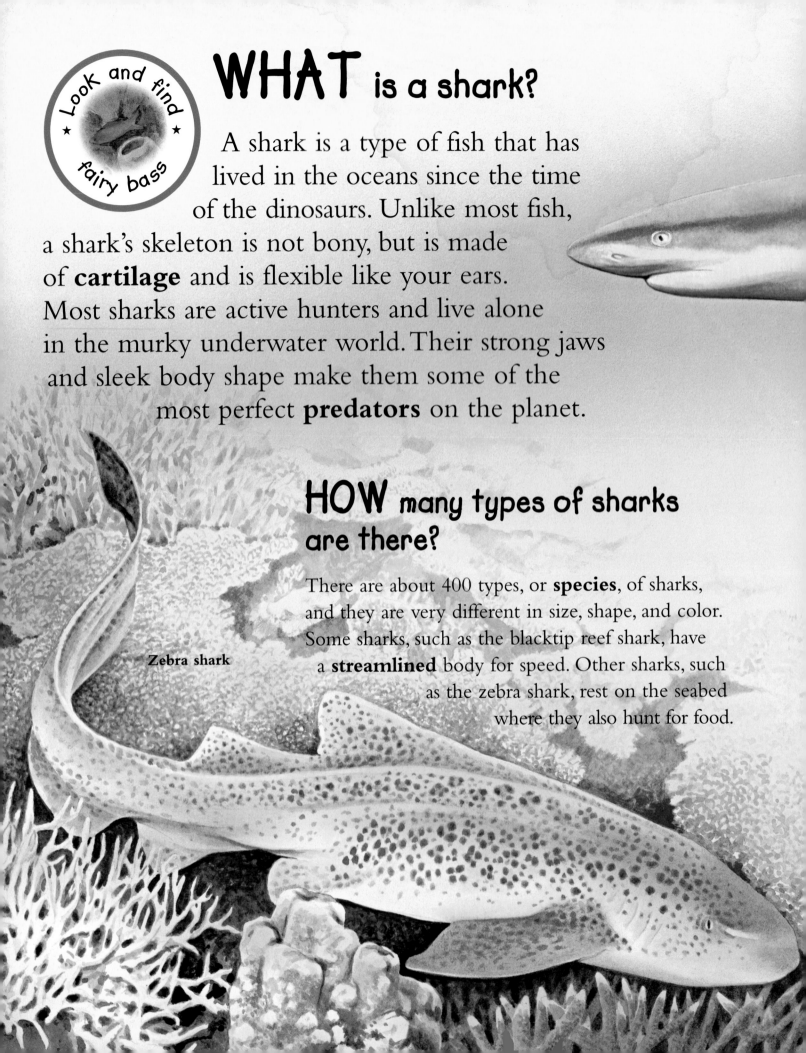

WHAT is a shark?

A shark is a type of fish that has lived in the oceans since the time of the dinosaurs. Unlike most fish, a shark's skeleton is not bony, but is made of **cartilage** and is flexible like your ears. Most sharks are active hunters and live alone in the murky underwater world. Their strong jaws and sleek body shape make them some of the most perfect **predators** on the planet.

HOW many types of sharks are there?

There are about 400 types, or **species**, of sharks, and they are very different in size, shape, and color. Some sharks, such as the blacktip reef shark, have a **streamlined** body for speed. Other sharks, such as the zebra shark, rest on the seabed where they also hunt for food.

Zebra shark

Blacktip reef shark

WHICH other fish are a type of shark?

Ray fish have a skeleton made of cartilage, so they are a type of shark. They have flat bodies with winglike fins and seem to fly through the water. Most rays have their mouths on the underside of their heads for eating animals living on the seabed.

That's amazing!

Ancient relatives of sharks lived in the oceans 400 million years ago!

Many small animals survive because sharks hunt the creatures that eat them!

Blue-spot ray

Now I know . . .

★ A shark is a type of fish with a skeleton made of cartilage.

★ There are about 400 types of sharks, which vary in size and shape.

★ Ray fish are a type of shark that have winglike fins.

WHERE do sharks live?

Sharks live in seas and oceans all over the world. Some species of sharks swim only in warm water, while others swim only in cold or cool water. They may live close to shore in the shallows or way out in the deep, open ocean. Some sharks live on the seabed where they rest or lie in wait for **prey** to swim near.

Fewer than 25 megamouths have been spotted since the discovery of this shark in 1976.

WHY does the megamouth live in the deep ocean?

The megamouth lives in the dark ocean depths where it is one of only a few creatures that eat **plankton** and jellyfish. This shark's large mouth is filled with small **organs** that glow, which may help attract its prey into its open mouth as it swims. Many strange-looking sharks live in the deep ocean. At 13 ft. (4m) long, the megamouth is the largest of these.

That's amazing!

A bull shark was seen in the Amazon River, 1,860 mi. (3,000km) from the ocean!

While many sharks live in warm tropical seas, the Greenland shark can survive in the icy waters of the Arctic Ocean!

Some bull sharks swim through rapids or very fast-moving water when traveling to and from Lake Nicaragua in Central America.

WHICH shark can live in rivers?

No type of shark can live in freshwater all the time. While a few sharks may swim a short distance up a river, they do not stay there very long. However, the bull shark can live far upriver for several weeks before returning to the sea. Bull sharks have been seen in many rivers, including the Congo in Africa, the Amazon in South America, and the Mississippi in the U.S.

Now I know . . .

★ Sharks are found in seas and oceans all over the world.
★ The megamouth feeds on plankton in the deep ocean.
★ The bull shark can live in rivers for several weeks.

HOW can a shark drown?

Sharks breathe by taking in **oxygen** from the water through their **gills**. Large sharks can breathe *only* when water flows past their gills. This means they have to keep swimming or they will stop breathing and drown. The smaller, bottom-dwelling sharks also breathe by pumping water over their gills, but they are able to do it resting on the seabed.

WHAT helps a great white shark keep swimming?

Many large sharks swim with side-to-side movements of their tails followed by a long, graceful glide to save energy. Unlike most sharks, a great white has a body temperature that is higher than the surrounding sea. This allows its swimming muscles to work better, so it can swim faster for longer.

WHICH shark is the greatest traveler?

Scientists have been able to find out which sharks travel the farthest. They attach small **tags** to the sharks and then record where they turn up. The blue shark holds the record for the longest distance traveled. Blue sharks often swim 1,200–2,000 mi. (2,000–3,000km) to **mate** or search for food. Scientists have also found that bottom-dwelling sharks often stay close to the area where they were born.

That's amazing!

A mako shark can leap out of the water at 22 mph (35km/h)!

A record-holding blue shark traveled 3,700 mi. (5,980km) from Brazil to New York!

Blue sharks normally swim alone, but several may appear together when there is a school of squids in one place.

Now I know . . .

★ Large sharks stop breathing and drown if they stop swimming.

★ A great white shark's high body temperature helps it swim faster for longer.

★ The blue shark is the greatest traveler.

9

Look and find tooth

HOW many rows of teeth do sandtiger sharks have?

Sandtiger sharks have as many as five rows of teeth. Only the teeth in the front row are used to catch and eat fish, octopuses, and small sharks. These front teeth often become damaged and fall out. When this happens, a tooth from the row behind moves forward to fill in the gap. This takes a few days. Sharks grow new teeth during their entire lives.

WHICH sharks have a really big bite?

Some large sharks, such as the great white shark, can push their jaws forward. This allows their jaws to open much wider so they can eat animals larger than their mouth. As the top jaw moves forward the lower jaw swings down. The shark then closes its mouth. The teeth of the lower jaw pierce and hold the prey, while the teeth of the upper jaw slice into it.

Great white shark opening its jaws to catch its prey

Sandtiger shark

WHY do sharks have different-shaped teeth?

Different shark species catch and eat different prey. The great white shark has triangular teeth with **serrated** edges for eating large animals, while the sandtiger shark has pointed teeth for grasping slippery prey. The gray nurse shark has grinding teeth for crushing shellfish.

Grinding teeth for crushing shellfish

Serrated tooth for eating large animals

Pointed tooth for catching slippery prey

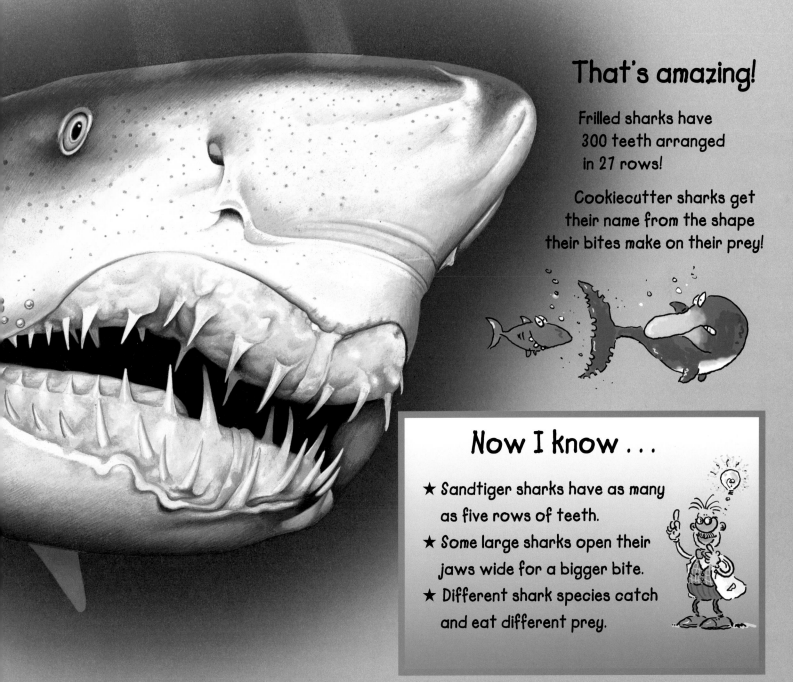

That's amazing!

Frilled sharks have 300 teeth arranged in 27 rows!

Cookiecutter sharks get their name from the shape their bites make on their prey!

Now I know . . .

★ Sandtiger sharks have as many as five rows of teeth.

★ Some large sharks open their jaws wide for a bigger bite.

★ Different shark species catch and eat different prey.

WHAT is a great white shark's favorite food?

A great white shark eats almost anything it catches, although seals are its favorite food. This includes the northern elephant seal, which can reach a massive 13 ft. (4m)—over half the length of the great white itself. Seals and sea lions are hard to catch, so the shark attacks them from below, racing up to the surface and catching them by surprise.

A great white shark can **breach**, or come right out of the sea, when it rushes up to the surface to catch a sea lion.

Sea lion

That's amazing!

An adult basking shark can filter 2,340 gal (9,000l) of seawater an hour!

Large sharks often swallow strange objects such as bottles, license plates, cans, and coats!

WHICH shark has the most varied diet?

The tiger shark has the most varied diet of any shark. It eats many different kinds of fish and even eats seabirds when they rest on the surface of the sea. A tiger shark's razor-sharp teeth can cut through the tough shells of sea turtles and horseshoe crabs. Young tiger sharks even eat very poisonous sea snakes.

HOW does a basking shark eat plankton?

The basking shark swims through the sea with its mouth wide open. Seawater enters its mouth and then passes out through its gills. Special bristles attached to the inside of its gills trap or **filter** out plankton from the water.

Basking shark swimming with its mouth open to catch plankton

Now I know . . .

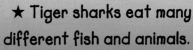

★ Seals are the great white shark's favorite food.

★ Tiger sharks eat many different fish and animals.

★ Basking sharks filter out plankton from seawater.

★ Look and find ★
pilot fish

HOW big is the whale shark?

The whale shark is the largest shark
and is bigger than any other fish.
Its average length is 45 ft. (14m)—
about half the size of a blue whale, the largest
mammal. Although the whale shark's mouth is
more than 3 feet (1m) wide, it eats only small
fish and tiny plankton. This enormous shark
is harmless to people and divers may
swim alongside it.

WHICH is the smallest shark?

The spiny pygmy shark is so small
it can fit on a human hand. The average
pygmy shark is just 8 inches (20cm) long.
This shark usually lives in the deep
ocean, but it swims close to the
surface of the ocean at night
to feed on small squid and fish.

A spiny pygmy shark—smaller than a hand

14

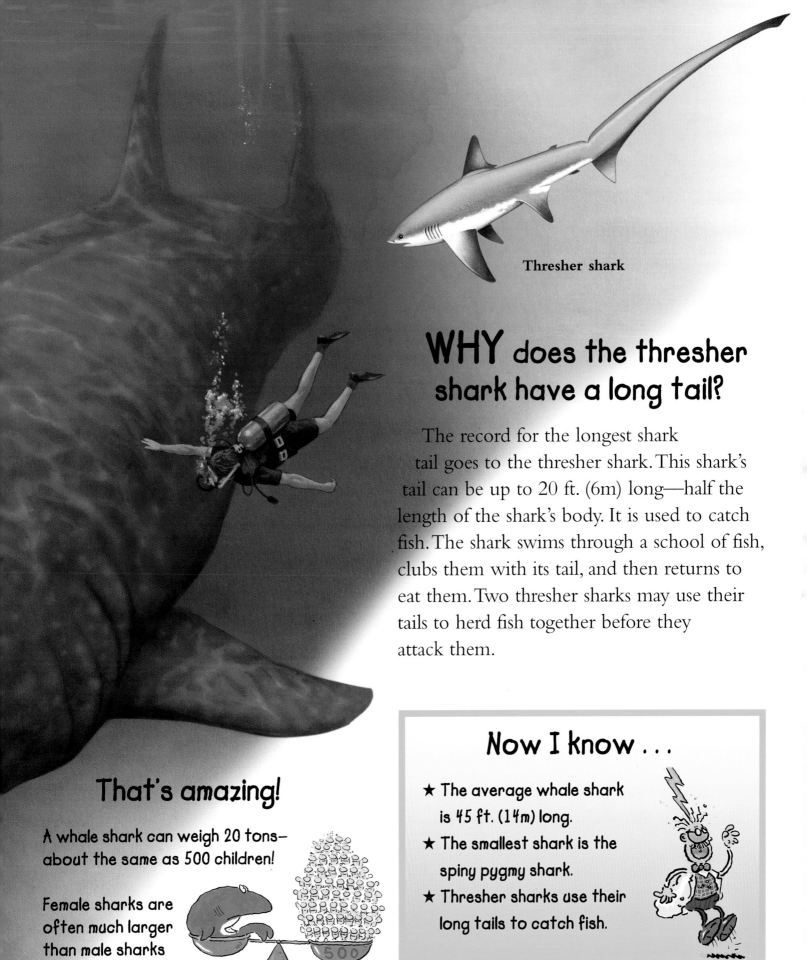

Thresher shark

WHY does the thresher shark have a long tail?

The record for the longest shark tail goes to the thresher shark. This shark's tail can be up to 20 ft. (6m) long—half the length of the shark's body. It is used to catch fish. The shark swims through a school of fish, clubs them with its tail, and then returns to eat them. Two thresher sharks may use their tails to herd fish together before they attack them.

That's amazing!

A whale shark can weigh 20 tons—about the same as 500 children!

Female sharks are often much larger than male sharks of the same species!

Now I know . . .

★ The average whale shark is 45 ft. (14m) long.
★ The smallest shark is the spiny pygmy shark.
★ Thresher sharks use their long tails to catch fish.

15

WHY are people frightened of sharks?

The life of a shark is mysterious and people are often afraid of things they do not understand. We know that some species of sharks attack people, and in our imaginations it is easy to turn them into scary monsters. In movies sharks are usually shown attacking people. In reality it is extremely rare for a shark to do this.

Tiger shark

That's amazing!

You are more likely to be struck by lightning than to be attacked by a shark!

The earliest recorded shark attack took place in 1580!

WHAT makes sharks attack people?

Sharks sometimes mistake people for their normal prey. When seen from below, a person lying on a surfboard looks like a seal or a turtle, and to a shark, the splashing movements of a swimmer sound like an injured animal. Sharks bite objects or people to taste them, but then often do not take another bite because they realize it is not their normal food.

WHICH sharks are not dangerous?

While all sharks should be treated with caution, most types of sharks rarely— if ever—attack people. This particularly includes the smaller, bottom-dwelling sharks. These smaller sharks attack only when they are disturbed by divers or if they are caught. They will also attack if they smell the blood of a fish that a diver has speared nearby.

Now I know . . .

★ People think sharks are scary monsters that attack people.
★ People are sometimes mistaken for a shark's normal prey.
★ Most sharks do not attack people and are not dangerous.

17

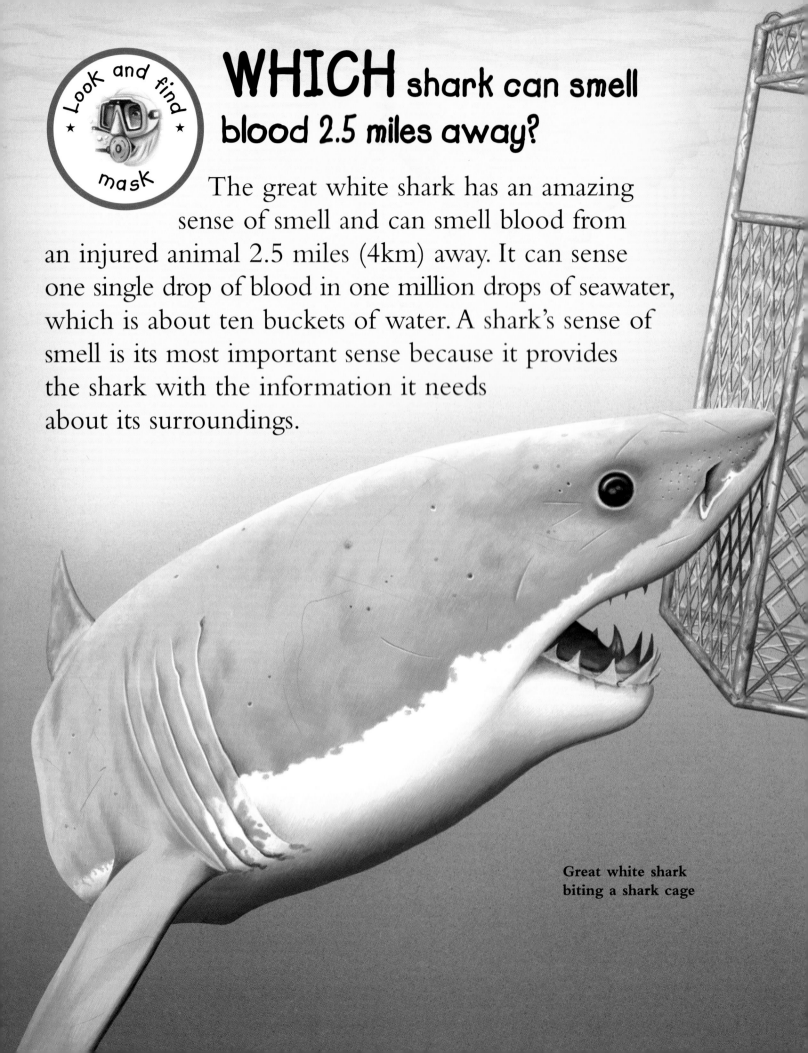

WHICH shark can smell blood 2.5 miles away?

The great white shark has an amazing sense of smell and can smell blood from an injured animal 2.5 miles (4km) away. It can sense one single drop of blood in one million drops of seawater, which is about ten buckets of water. A shark's sense of smell is its most important sense because it provides the shark with the information it needs about its surroundings.

Great white shark biting a shark cage

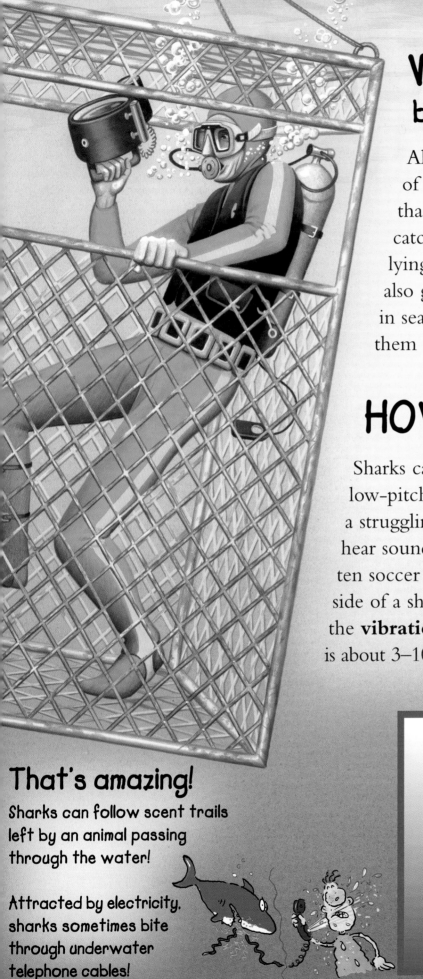

WHY do sharks bite shark cages?

All living things produce a small amount of electricity. Sharks have an unusual sense that detects this electricity and helps them catch prey that is close to them, even if it is lying still under the sand. Most metal objects also give off a small amount of electricity in seawater. This can confuse sharks and cause them to bite metal objects, such as shark cages.

HOW do sharks hear?

Sharks can hear very well, especially deep, low-pitched sounds such as those produced by a struggling, injured animal. They may be able to hear sounds as far away as 1,000 yards—roughly ten soccer fields. Special **sensory cells** on the side of a shark's body and head also pick up the **vibrations** made by an animal that is about 3–10 ft. (1–3m) away.

That's amazing!

Sharks can follow scent trails left by an animal passing through the water!

Attracted by electricity, sharks sometimes bite through underwater telephone cables!

Now I know . . .

★ Great white sharks can smell blood 2.5 mi. (4km) away.
★ Sharks think shark cages are prey and attack them.
★ Sharks can hear very well—especially low-pitched sounds.

19

WHY are most sharks gray and white?

Most sharks have a dark gray back with a white underside. This is a type of **camouflage** called countershading, which helps a shark hunt its prey and attack without being seen. When a shark is seen from above, its dark back is hidden by the shadowy water below it. When looked at from underneath, a shark's white belly blends in with the bright surface of the water.

That's amazing!

In the past, sharkskin was used as sandpaper!

Sharkskin is used to make purses, shoes, and wallets. The toothlike scales are scraped off first!

Gray reef shark

Pilot fish

WHAT makes sharkskin rough?

Instead of having slippery scales like most other fish, a shark's body is covered in tiny, toothlike scales. These scales make sharkskin very rough and protect a shark's body like a suit of armor. The scales also make the shark's body more streamlined, so it can swim with ease through the water.

WHICH shark's skin helps it blend into the seabed?

Sharks that live on the seabed have skin colors that camouflage them from the sea creatures they eat. The wobbegong's body is covered in colorful splotches, spots, and lines. These patterns help it easily blend in with the seabed, where it lies and waits to catch passing fish, octopuses, crabs, and lobsters.

The wobbegong shark has tassels around its mouth that look like seaweed. This helps camouflage the shark.

Now I know . . .

★ Most sharks are gray and white to help camouflage them.

★ Sharkskin is covered in tiny, toothlike scales.

★ The wobbegong shark's skin helps it blend in with the seabed.

★ Look and find ★
mouth

WHICH shark has a hammer?

No one really knows why the hammerhead shark has a head shaped like a hammer. The shark's nostrils are farther apart, which may help it pinpoint the direction of a smell. It may also sharpen the shark's sense that uses electricity to find prey. The shape of its head may also help the shark turn and move up and down quickly.

HOW does the sawshark catch fish?

The sawshark has a flattened body and a snout with needle-sharp teeth along the edges. This makes a dangerous weapon for catching prey or for defense. The sawshark moves its head sideways, slashing into its prey or enemy. The snout can also stir up the sandy seabed to uncover prey such as shrimp. It uses its feelers to find other animals under the sand.

Sawshark searching the seabed with its feelers

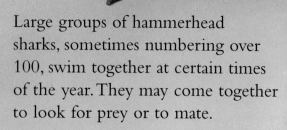

Large groups of hammerhead sharks, sometimes numbering over 100, swim together at certain times of the year. They may come together to look for prey or to mate.

22

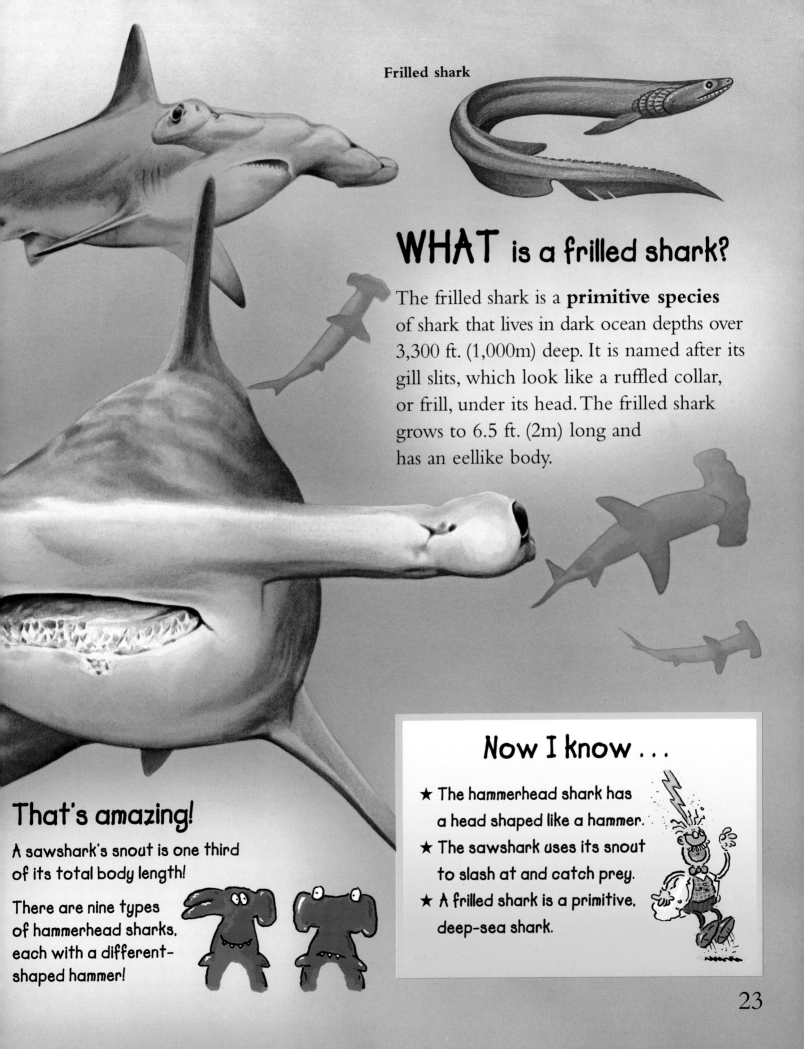

Frilled shark

WHAT is a frilled shark?

The frilled shark is a **primitive species** of shark that lives in dark ocean depths over 3,300 ft. (1,000m) deep. It is named after its gill slits, which look like a ruffled collar, or frill, under its head. The frilled shark grows to 6.5 ft. (2m) long and has an eellike body.

That's amazing!

A sawshark's snout is one third of its total body length!

There are nine types of hammerhead sharks, each with a different-shaped hammer!

Now I know . . .

★ The hammerhead shark has a head shaped like a hammer.
★ The sawshark uses its snout to slash at and catch prey.
★ A frilled shark is a primitive, deep-sea shark.

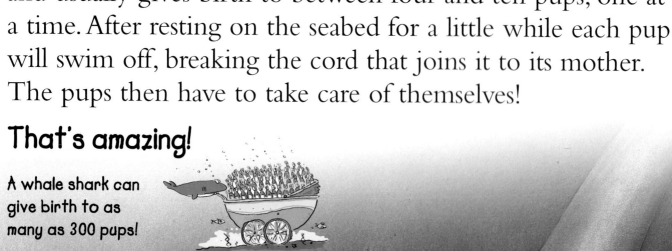

Look and find ★ ★ fin

HOW are lemon sharks born?

A female lemon shark gives birth to young called pups that have grown inside her for several months. She swims into shallow water and usually gives birth to between four and ten pups, one at a time. After resting on the seabed for a little while each pup will swim off, breaking the cord that joins it to its mother. The pups then have to take care of themselves!

That's amazing!

A whale shark can give birth to as many as 300 pups!

While still in its mother's body, a baby gray nurse shark will attack and eat its unborn brothers and sisters!

Cord joining the pup to its mother

24

WHICH sharks lay eggs?

Some small sharks, such as dogfish, cat sharks, carpet sharks, and horn sharks, lay 20 to 25 eggs at a time. Each egg is protected inside a special egg case, which is either attached to seaweed or hidden on the seabed. The baby shark will grow inside the egg case. The shark feeds from the **yolk sac** attached to its body. It will hatch after several months.

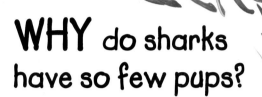

WHY do sharks have so few pups?

Many fish lay thousands of eggs, but most of the fish that hatch do not survive because they are eaten by other fish. However, most sharks only need to produce a few eggs. These develop inside the mother or in an egg case. When sharks are born or hatch, they are much bigger than many other fish, so most avoid being eaten.

Hammerhead shark pups

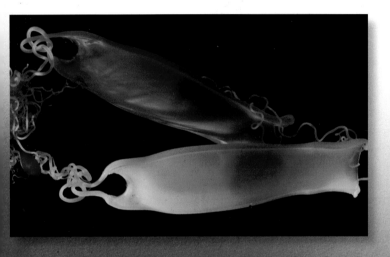

Dogfish attached to yolk sac in an egg case

Now I know . . .

★ Baby lemon shark pups develop inside their mother.
★ Some small sharks lay eggs protected by egg cases.
★ Sharks produce large young that can avoid being eaten.

Lemon shark pup swimming away from its mother

25

WHY do pilot fish live with sharks?

The black-and-white striped pilot fish lives with several large sea creatures, including sharks. When living close to a shark, pilot fish are less likely to be eaten by other predators. They can also snap up small scraps of food when a shark is feeding. However, the pilot fish must remain alert or they may also become part of a shark's meal.

Whitetip reef shark

Pilot fish

Remora fish

HOW does a remora fish hitch a ride on a shark?

When swimming next to a shark the remora fish, or shark sucker, is pulled along by the shark's movement through the water. However, it can also attach itself to the shark using a special sucker on top of its head. Three types of remoras live with sharks, feeding off of the **parasites** that live on sharkskin.

WHICH fish help sharks?

Several fish help sharks by feeding on tiny parasites that live on sharkskin. Fish such as the barber fish are usually found in areas of coral reefs known as cleaning stations. Sharks and other large fish swim slowly around these areas so that the fish from the cleaning stations can come out and pick off their parasites. Cleaner fish are never eaten by the sharks.

A barber fish cleaning a hammerhead shark

That's amazing!

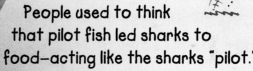

Remora fish attach themselves to any large moving object, such as boats, whales, sharks, and even divers!

People used to think that pilot fish led sharks to food—acting like the sharks "pilot."

Now I know . . .

★ Being close to a shark protects pilot fish from being eaten.

★ A remora fish sticks onto a shark using a sucker.

★ Several species of fish feed off of parasites that live on sharks.

Look and find ★ ★ tern

WHO eats sharks?

A few large predators such as killer whales will eat sharks, and large sharks sometimes eat smaller sharks. However, people eat more sharks than any sea predator. People who live near the sea have always eaten shark meat, but the meat is now popular worldwide. This is mainly because the usual supply of fish meat, such as cod, is in danger as a result of overfishing.

WHY are many sharks endangered?

People kill around 100 million sharks every year. Some are fished for food while others, such as basking sharks, are caught for their oil. Sharkskin is made into boots and teeth are used in jewelry. Many sharks also die when caught accidentally in fishing nets. Today up to 80 percent of shark species are endangered. Their numbers may never recover because sharks produce only a few young.

A mako shark tries to free itself from a fishing line by leaping out of the water

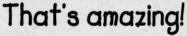

That's amazing!

In some parts of the world people eat sharkfin soup!

The dogfish shark, also called rock salmon, is one of the fish eaten in British "fish and chips"!

Shark jaws are kept as trophies by fishermen who hunt sharks as a sport. Jaws are also sold to tourists.

HOW can people protect sharks?

To protect sharks people must stop killing them as a sport and realize their important role in the oceans' food chain and in the balance of the sea population. Scientists tag sharks to study their movements and keep track of their numbers. In this way we may be able to save sharks from becoming **extinct**.

Now I know . . .

★ People eat more sharks than any other predator.
★ People kill 100 million sharks every year.
★ We can help protect sharks by studying them and charting their movements.

SHARKS QUIZ

What have you remembered
about sharks? Test what you know,
and see how much you have learned.

1 Where do zebra sharks hunt for food?
a)   in rivers
b)   in the deep ocean
c)   on the seabed

2 Why do scientists tag sharks?
a)   to reduce shark attacks
b)   to track distances traveled
c)   to measure them

3 What is made of cartilage?
a)   shark cage
b)   shark tag
c)   shark skeleton

4 Which shark can have 300 young?
a)   blue shark
b)   whale shark
c)   lemon shark

5 Which fish sticks to sharks?
a)   remora fish
b)   ray fish
c)   barber fish

6 Why does the sandtiger shark have pointed teeth?
a)   to crush shellfish
b)   to eat large animals
c)   to grasp slippery prey

7 What does the pygmy shark eat?
a)   plankton
b)   small squids and fish
c)   seals

8 Which is a shark's most important sense?
a)   smell
b)   touch
c)   sight

9 Where does the frilled shark live?
a)   shallow water
b)   dark ocean depths
c)   rivers

10 How many sharks do people kill each year?
a)   One thousand
b)   100 thousand
c)   100 million

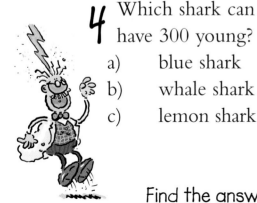

Find the answers on page 32.

GLOSSARY

breach To jump up out of the water and fall back down with a splash.

camouflage To be colored in order to blend in with the surrounding area.

cartilage A light, flexible material that makes up a shark's skeleton. Your ears are made of cartilage.

extinct No longer living on earth. An animal becomes extinct when not one of its type survives.

filter To separate food from substances such as water.

gills Tiny featherlike parts inside slits behind a shark's eyes. Sharks breathe in oxygen through their gills when water passes over or into them.

mate When a male and a female of the same kind come together to breed and, as a result, produce young.

organs Parts of the body that carry out different roles. The megamouth has small organs in its mouth that give off light.

oxygen A gas in the air and in water; all animals need to breathe in oxygen to live.

parasites Creatures that live on or in other creatures. Parasites can harm and irritate the creature they live on.

plankton Tiny creatures and plants that live in the sea.

predators Animals that hunt other animals for food.

prey Animals that are hunted and killed by other animals.

primitive species A species that has existed for thousands of years, before many other species developed.

sensory cells A line of sensitive areas along the length of a shark's body in the skin. They help a shark sense tiny movements in the water around them.

serrated Having a sharp, zig-zagged edge like that of a saw.

species A type of plant or animal.

streamlined Having a smooth body shape that moves easily through air or water.

tags Small plastic labels containing electronic chips that give out signals scientists can follow. Tags are clipped onto sharks' fins—this does not hurt the shark.

vibrations When something moves in water, the movement shakes the area around it and causes wavelike motions called vibrations.

yolk sac A pouch of thin skin in an egg case that contains yolk, a liquid that provides food for a developing creature.

INDEX

A

Arctic Ocean 7
attacks on people 16, 17

B

barber fish 27
basking sharks 13, 28
birth 24, 25
blacktip reef sharks 4, 5
blue sharks 9
body shape 4, 5, 22, 23
breaching 12, 31
breathing 8, 9
bull sharks 7

C

camouflage 20, 21, 31
carpet sharks 25
cartilage 4, 5, 31
cat sharks 25
color 4, 20, 21
cookiecutter sharks 11

D

divers 14, 17, 27
dogfish sharks 25, 28

E

eggs 25

electricity 19, 22
endangered species 28–29
extinction 29, 31

F

filtering 13, 31
fins 5, 24
fishing industry 28, 29
food 4, 5, 6, 9, 10, 11, 12,
   13, 14, 21, 22, 26, 27, 28
frilled sharks 11, 23

G

gills 8, 13, 23, 31
great white sharks 8, 9, 10,
   11, 12, 13, 18, 19
Greenland sharks 7
gray nurse sharks 11, 24
gray reef sharks 20

H

hammerhead sharks 22,
   23, 25, 27
hearing 19
horn sharks 25
hunting 4, 5, 6, 10, 11, 12,
   14, 15, 17, 18, 19, 20, 21,
   22, 23

J

jaws 4, 10, 11, 29

L

lemon sharks 24, 25

M

mako sharks 9, 28
mating 9, 22, 31
megamouth sharks 6, 7

O

ocean depths 6, 7, 14, 23
octopus 10, 16, 21
oxygen 8, 31

P

parasites 26, 27, 31
pilot fish 14, 26, 27
plankton 6, 7, 13, 14, 31
predators 4, 26, 28, 29, 31
pups 24, 25

R

rays 5
remora fish 26, 27
rivers 7

S

sandtiger sharks 10, 11
saw sharks 22, 23
sea lions 12
seabed 4, 5, 6, 8, 21, 22,
   24, 25
sensory cells 19, 31
shark cages 18, 19
shark meat 28
size 4, 5, 6, 14, 15, 23,
   24, 25, 28
skeletons 4, 5

skin 20, 21, 26, 27, 28
smell 18, 19, 22
speed 4, 8, 9
spiny pygmy sharks 14, 15
streamlining 4, 21, 31
swimming 5, 6, 8, 9, 13,
   21, 22, 26, 27

T

tagging 9, 29, 31
tail 8, 15
teeth 10–11, 13, 22, 28
temperature, body 8, 9
thresher sharks 15
tiger sharks 13, 16
traveling 9

W

whale sharks 14, 15, 24
whitetip reef sharks 26
wobbegong sharks 21

Z

zebra sharks 4

Answers to the Sharks Quiz on page 30

★ 1 c ★ 2 b ★ 3 c ★ 4 b ★ 5 a ★ 6 c ★ 7 b ★ 8 a ★ 9 b ★ 10 c